Test planning with TMMi practices

Assuring the quality by applying Continuous test planning methods with TMMi practices.

Author: Shanthi Vemulapalli

Version 1.0

Copyright 2015

Table of contents

In continuation of my previous book on TMMi practices titled:
"Following TMMi practices to produce Quality software
products" a kindle edition with more emphasize on Test policy
and strategy, I am continuing the TMMi practices for Level2
practices following.

For the above E-book you can click on the below link:

https://www.createspace.com/5894426

The reader is advised to read the Test policy and strategy
process before reading this Book for easy understanding.

As a part of recollection of TMMi and CMMi mapping KPAs let use the below chart:

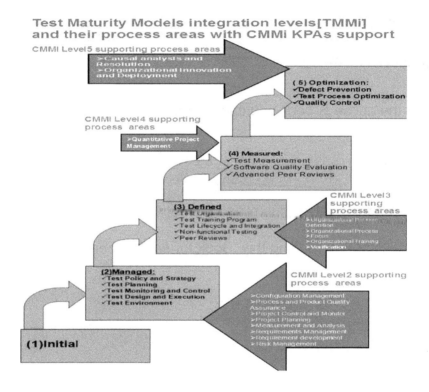

Test Maturity Models integration levels[TMMi] and their process areas with CMMi KPAs support

In this Book I have considered the TMMi level2 process area on "Test planning" to elaborate with different examples while considering to implement those practices.

The reader is advised to go through the website: www.tmmifoundation.org for its framework and other guidelines from the PDF document: "The overall structure of the TMMi Reference Model including details of each level."

For every Process area of sub-process they need to refer the TMMi framework book from the foundation site. That has been considered as a guide while elaborating the process steps in this book with examples.

I would like to denote the KPAs through process charts or figures drawn by me, against to each KPA while moving to co-relate them for live examples.

Many testing professionals either junior or senior might think test planning is nothing but writing the test plan either with an Excel template or if some of them are slightly advanced or matured in test process; they might think just filling the IEEE 829 template and circulate for a review or sign-off. These were my past close observations with many test managers and leads.

In reality; the test planning is an ongoing activity till the Software build is released to the production by getting the sign-off from the business sponsor or the relevant application software's user group head.

The movement the software release is planned onwards; the testing team or the test management team need to keep working on test planning and re-planning on their activities. Once the initial plan sign of is done, definitely there might be changes for the application in this dynamic business and technology trends or scenarios, to have continuous test re-planning activity towards smooth functioning of testing activities.

Hence the test management activity is an ongoing activity in several areas of the software releases. The release can be followed with any development or test methodology, but test planning should be there till the release sign-off happened successfully with their customer satisfaction.

Many testing professionals cannot identify the required test planning activity at different stages of the project. The reason might be the testing organization may not be matured enough to follow some of the better or strategic processes or practices. In such case definitely the blame on "rolling the wrong product to production" would be owned by the testing team, even though the testing team members worked hard or being burnt day and night including week-ends for numerous test phases and their test cycles for a software release.

Let us recap the process areas for TMMi Level2 with the below Chart:

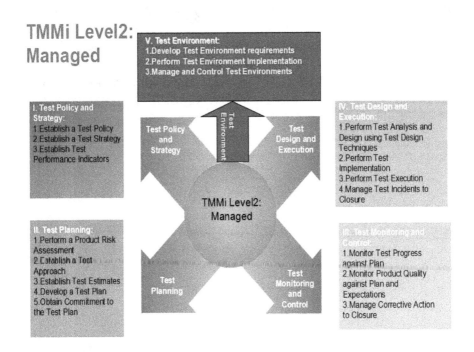

TMMi Level2: Managed

V. Test Environment:
1.Develop Test Environment requirements
2.Perform Test Environment Implementation
3.Manage and Control Test Environments

I. Test Policy and Strategy:
1.Establish a Test Policy
2.Establish a Test Strategy
3.Establish Test Performance Indicators

Test Policy and Strategy

Test Environment

Test Design and Execution

IV. Test Design and Execution:
1.Perform Test Analysis and Design using Test Design Techniques
2.Perform Test Implementation
3.Perform Test Execution
4.Manage Test Incidents to Closure

TMMi Level2: Managed

II. Test Planning:
1.Perform a Product Risk Assessment
2.Establish a Test Approach
3.Establish Test Estimates
4.Develop a Test Plan
5.Obtain Commitment to the Test Plan

Test Planning

Test Monitoring and Control

III. Test Monitoring and Control:
1.Monitor Test Progress against Plan
2.Monitor Product Quality against Plan and Expectations
3.Manage Corrective Action to Closure

To reduce the testing team efforts and create a matured testing organization, the TMMi Level2 practices helps the professionals to have a structured test planning activity. By following these practices it not only educate the teams and also helps to achieve the quality software products within the planned schedule to a testing organization.

While adopting these practices incrementally, one can keep learning their advantages and also the team's maturity levels acceleration. We need to consider the TMMi test planning process activity implementation as; it is going to reduce the product malfunctioning performance risks incrementally. At the same time the Testing organization also can get commitment and dedication from different stakeholders.

Chapter 3: Overview of Test planning Practices areas

As per the TMMi Test planning process area [PA], it consists of the following specific goals [GA]:

Performing product risk assessment, Establishing a test approach,

Establishing test estimates, Developing a test plan, Obtaining the commitment for the test plan.

The Test Planning is:

To define a test approach based on the identified risks and the defined test Strategy.

To establish and maintain well-founded plans for performing and managing the testing activities. Once the test assignment is confirmed, the overall study should be carried out regarding the: Product to be tested, Project organization, Requirements, Development process.

The test plan document template should be followed as per the *IEEE 829 standards.*

Now, you have seen the activities involved in the test planning from the above chart.

Now let us see, what should be the test organization policy?

Following points should be considered for test organization

policy making: The Organization should *establish and*

maintain an organizational policy for planning and performing

the Test Planning process or activities. The typical test

planning policy could include the following:

A test plan should be defined for each project.

The project's test approach should be derived from the test

strategy.

The test plans should be complied with a pre-defined

process and template.

The tools will be used during the test planning for different

projects should be mentioned.

The project relevant test requirements should be

mentioned.

The test estimates and the relevant cost for budget

planning need to be identified.

The negotiation should happen on testing commitments

with the resource management, business management

and the project management teams.

The involvement of different groups during test planning should be mentioned.

The test plan management and the controls should be defined.

Finally, the management should review defined policies with reference to their commitments made and also as per the organization standards.

As per the TMMi Test planning process area; each of the above Specific goals have been sub-divided into different specific practices [SP] areas as per the TMMi framework.

The following chart has the decomposed Test planning

process area into its specific practices:

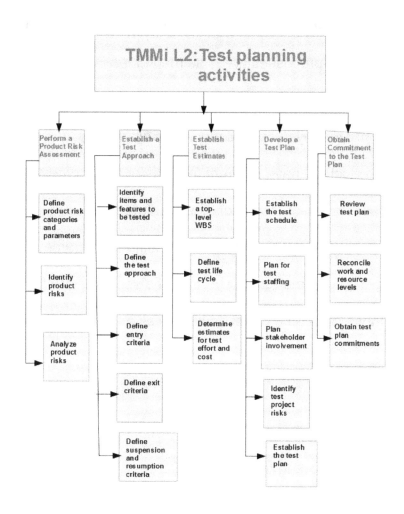

TMMi L2: Test planning activities

- **Perform a Product Risk Assessment**
  - Define product risk categories and parameters
  - Identify product risks
  - Analyze product risks

- **Establish a Test Approach**
  - Identify items and features to be tested
  - Define the test approach
  - Define entry criteria
  - Define exit criteria
  - Define suspension and resumption criteria

- **Establish Test Estimates**
  - Establish a top-level WBS
  - Define test life cycle
  - Determine estimates for test effort and cost

- **Develop a Test Plan**
  - Establish the test schedule
  - Plan for test staffing
  - Plan stakeholder involvement
  - Identify test project risks
  - Establish the test plan

- **Obtain Commitment to the Test Plan**
  - Review test plan
  - Reconcile work and resource levels
  - Obtain test plan commitments

For every software product testing, the experienced professional can assess the relevant risks. This Specific Goal has three sub-processes areas as mentioned in the above chart.

Define product risk categories and parameters:

Each product will have different features or areas of testing. While assessing for testing of these features, we can classify them under different categories by defining the parameters of testing. The parameters can be part of a scenario or a test case those can come under its criteria also.

Example:

Let us assume a Bank ATM application. It needs to have a simulated network to test the ATM Cards. And the screen display with touch pad options.

These functional areas can come under infrastructure and the application architecture areas. They are;

a) ATM Machine,

b) Card reader,

c) Printer [inside the machine], etc.

Now let us see the risks; the relevant risk items can be along with their categories A, B, C;

 A) ATM screen display is not working,

B) Card reader is not working,

C) It doesn't give printout.

By considering the priorities and these functions importance for customer;

The risk levels can be for these categories; A- high, B-high, C-low.

If you prioritize them for testing; A should be on priority 1, B should be on priority 1, C should be on priority 3.

This way we can decompose the product application's features to identify different risks for decomposed functions also. Now we can prepare the testing risk register to track their closure or contingency handling.

Identify product risks:

We need to identify the risks during the planning stage. These risks identification need to be an ongoing activity till the release SIGN-OFF happens.

Example:

From the above example we can consider the below as product risks:

Risk1: ATM Machine functioning,

Risk2: Card reader functioning,

Risk3: Functioning of Receipt printout.

Analyze product risks:

Any identified risk should be analyzed on its impact to different areas of the project or to the business when the product is deployed into live. Similar way the above identified risks can be analyzed.

Example:

Risk1: ATM Machine functioning: If the ATM machine is not functioning the bank customers can no withdraw the money. Customer revisit can reduce and they can opt for other Banks. The alternate plans should be made available to serve to the customers.

Risk2: Card reader functioning: If the card the card reader is not functioning, it is as good as ATM machine is not working. The same analysis can be arrived for this risk also.

Risk3: Functioning of Receipt printout: If the printout is not coming, the bank can assume the display is working to show the balance to the customer after the money is disbursed from the ATM machine. This can compensate without loosing the customer from the bank. In this case we do not need to have immediate contingency, and the team can consider to fix the defect. The defect can be there is not paper in the ATM printer or there can be software defect to print it. or even sometimes the paper might get struck in the ATM printer.

Brainstorm sessions for risks identification:

These are the possible ways one need to identify to analyze the risks. But unless the testing team has in-depth product knowledge it is very difficult to identify the risks. Hence it is very essential to have brainstorming sessions with the business users since they are well versed on the past live issues, they will be able to give some thoughts to identify the product risks. Also they will be able to identify the risk category, priority, level, etc.

Note on risk register:

With all the sub-process areas we have done the risk assessment as per the "**Perform a Product Risk Assessment** " process area. Now a risk register need to be maintained to record all the above identified risks, categories, test parameters, risk analysis, etc. Further these can be used for contingency plans or actions.

In general to test any product feature, we need to follow an approach which is called test approach. This test approach can change from one test scenario to another scenario. Hence each product feature can have its own test approach also or it can be combined with another scenario or sub-scenario.

Example:

Let us consider the ATM features testing example.

We need decompose the ATM test scenario into the following sub features:

Testing the card acceptance

Testing the amount transaction and its updates in the account with the latest balance.

Testing the Receipt printout

Even if it has SMS option for balance communication it should be considered.

If we consider any of the there is not common approach to test or evaluate the functionality. At the same time, if any of the features are failing in the middle we need to have where to close the test and restart it again when the defect is fixed for the new build.

Identify items and features to be tested

Each product should have multiple features or functionalities. These need to be decomposed into low level testable items.

Example:

If we consider the ATM examples discussed in the above section, we have decomposed them into four testable features. But each of them will have still low level items to be verified.

Let us consider one of them;

i. Testing the card acceptance. It should be divided or decomposed into different parts verification:

a)   Testing the PIN to access the card. With right and wrong pin.

b)   Testing the available balance before we use for the transaction on ATM display.

Similar way every product can have its features to be tested and they should be decomposed into testable low level items.

Now let us see the sub-processes; Defining test approach, Define entry criteria, Define entry criteria, Define exit criteria and Define suspension and resumption criteria.

Define the test approach

As discussed in the previous sections, every feature need to have a test approach identified in the beginning. And the approach should contain the low level information validation approach also.

Example:

Let us consider the ATM scenario's function: Testing ATM Card.

Our main test scenario can be: Verify the ATM card for its account allocated correctness.

The test approach can be; a) Insert the right ATM card and use the right pin to verify the available balance. In this description we are not giving the card number or pin#. It is a general test approach to test the right ATM card.

Now the negative test approach can be two ways one is enter wrong ATM pin and test it. Use the wrong ATM card and test it.

This way we should be able to identify the test approaches for different functions of any product.

Define entry criteria

For every product testing we need to have any entry criteria. The entry criteria can be the software build readiness which is installed and setup for its usage.

Sometimes, we need to use the startup test scenarios; in general they are called as smoke test scenarios.

Example:

If we take ATM scenario, we need to have a test lab with ATM machine or machines setup with their network connected for the test software servers. This setup can be one of the test entry criteria. Then you also need the right and wrong ATM cards along with their account details under test data readiness. If any of them are not ready, we can not start the testing.

Define exit criteria

For every test completion there is an exit criteria. There can be a series of features need to be planned and once they all are passed the test exit or closure can be announced. These need to be identified upfront before going for test execution.

Example:

In case of ATM testing we can have the exit criteria. As we have identified the features and test items to be tested, those all need to be passed to complete the testing. Then only we can announce the test exit.

Define suspension and resumption criteria

For every test cycle there is entry criteria and exit criteria as we have discussed in the above sections. In all possible ways if we consider in our first attempt the test completion or exit is not going to happen, there should be test suspension criteria and resumption criteria.

The test suspension defines when and how to suspend the testing depends on the allowed defects. These items need to be identified during test planning itself.

Similarly, once the identified defects are fixed and next test cycle is planned the test resumption criteria need to be planned.

Let us see the example.

Example: From the identified ATM test scenarios, let us consider the ATM receipt printout. When we are testing the printout we know its show stoppers as; i) Paper struck in ATM printer, ii) Software defect. Let us assume any one of them are identified we are suppose to stop the testing and fix the defect to retest and certify its function, once this defect is identified.

Assume, the ATM account is already had a withdrawal transaction in the account when this test was failed. In such case when the defect is fixed it is ready for retesting, the resumption criteria should have "The resting need to start with the new transaction". This can give clarity to the testers and also to the users on how to restart the testing.

The similar way for every feature failure we should have clarity on how to suspend the testing and on how to restart or resume the testing along with its required test data. In ATM example we can use the right and wrong ATM cards. For other applications the team needs to identify the similar items.

By now, assuming the reader might have got a good clarity on the sub-processes of; Defining test approach, Define entry criteria, Define entry criteria, Define exit criteria and Define suspension and resumption criteria, from the above live examples.

For every testing project, the testing team needs to identify the product test scenarios or its main functionalities. These need to be decomposed into different sub-scenarios or sub-functionalities. Then the test team members need to be allocated to keep working on these test items test planning. One of the testing activities is to estimate the efforts of the testing activities. The team needs to drill down the activities into tasks. Then they need to work on the sequences of these test items to be performed for test execution.

When we consider the above situations, the following activities or tasks are mandatory for a testing professional to perform, as TMMi also suggests following as sub-processes under the goal of "Establish Test Estimates":

Establishing a top-level work breakdown structure

Defining test life-cycle

Determining estimates for test efforts and cost

Before planning these activities you need to make sure the testing team members are planned for different functionalities. And they are brainstormed for these product features.

Establish a top-level work breakdown structure

When we do any project planning, we need to find its different activities. And drill down them into sub-activities. These sub-activities can be decomposed into tasks and sub-tasks. Before doing this decomposition, we also need to find the scope of the project. With the scope we will be able to concentrate on those areas of the project and it helps to find the work breakdown upto its sub-tasks.

Similarly in any testing project, the work breakdown structure [WBS] need to be defined clearly before Test estimate stage. Once the WBS is identified for the entire project, it can give clarity on further planning process also.

Example:

In our ATM testing project example, we can have the below WBS.

c) Testing ATM Card

c.1 Testing the ATM Card

1.1.1 Testing the right and wrong pin for ATM card

d) Verify the account authentication

2.1 Checking the balance towards access of correct account

2.1.1 Verify the display screen for the amount

2.1.2 Issuing the receipt printout

2.1.3 Verify the balance from the receipt.

You can see the detailed WBS into low level test requirements.

The similar way for any project we should be able to decompose the WBS, if you have taken a product functionality orientation for project team members before test planning.

From the above product items list the team members should be able to plan their activities against to the WBS task, as per their internal setup by following the policies. [Please refer to the test policy module to know its details].

Define test life-cycle

When we attempt to test any function or feature of a software project, it will have sequence of testing.

Example:

By considering the ATM test scenario. We have seen from the previous examples in different sections the ATM has the sequence of test execution steps.

Without inserting the right ATM card, by not feeding the right ATM pin one can not see the current balance. We need to follow the sequence of the several test items.

The sequence of these test items need to be defined under ATM test life-cycle.

The similar way any product function can be considered to define a test life-cycle.

It can also give clarity to the team members to plan the structured testing and to break the code also to find defects.

Determine estimates for test effort and cost

As we have seen from the above sections under test estimate goal, we found the sub-tasks also for a product. And also through them each team member has been allocated. And these team members need to plan their activities by keeping allocated functionalities verification. Once they found their detailed work for different test activities, they need to estimate all of them for their effort.

Once all the team found the required efforts, the test management needs to estimate the resources costing for the test project.

Example:

If you consider the ATM test cycle, the team found its test items and they also can identify some more hidden efforts under different activities. All of them they need to consider for their effort estimation. From those efforts the test management can assess the resources costing for different activities of the project.

Note on Test estimates:

After understanding the test estimates sub-process areas, it is very evident from top to bottom of within the team structure the product functions understanding into low level is very essential.

Their dependencies and the required support need to be considered for different project activities apart from the regular test activities like, documentation, reviews, test data, environment, test execution, defects tracking, test closure, etc.

This way it can help to have a full control on the test management also.

Every testing project will have a test plan. It is useful to manage the testing project and also to communicate to different stakeholder at each activity of testing what the team is planned to do. For tracking purpose for the management it is essential to maintain the test plan.

The popular test plan template is from IEE 829 standard. The reader is advised to look into that template while going through this chapter.

As per the TMMi Develop Test plan goal, it has the below specific process areas:

Establish the test schedule

Plan for test staffing

Plan stakeholder involvement

Identify test project risks

Establish the test plan

From the above processes; it is required to plan and develop a test schedule. And plan for test resources. Get the stakeholder involvement. Identifying the test project risks. And developing the test plan by using the IEEE 829 Standards.

On some of these processes we might get some idea from the examples we have discussed in previous sections.
Now let us see each of these processes with the relevant examples.

Establish the test schedule:
Let us recollect from Test estimate processes. We have seen the test items and also the relevant test life cycle for functionality. Different test team members have been groomed for the functionalities allocated to them as per the scenarios discussed. By using these we need to plan for a test schedule.

Assuming by now the team members are aware of their activities from previous sections elaboration and the activities planned by them. Now those need to be identified and allocate a task for each of them with start and end date.

We should give liberty to the team members to come up with the reasonable schedule. They are well aware by now how much optimal time they need to perform each of those tasks. Whatever tasks/sub-tasks they have identified it is better to put them in the schedule for easy tracking purpose. This can help if anybody got struck while executing the sub-task; it can be tracked for the show stoppers and can be resolved faster. Since the individuals planning are made through the estimates and other processes, it is very for them also to look into the current issues and explain to the management.

Example:

Assuming the below are the some of the tasks/sub-tasks can be used for ATM test scenario.

1.   ATM test environment readiness

2.   Writing test approach and test strategy for ATM scenario.

3.   Developing test cases for Card operation.

4.   Developing test data for ATM cards.

5.   Review of test approach and test strategy

6.   Updates of test approach and test strategy

7.   Review of test cases

8.   Updates of test cases

9.   Test execution for ATM cards testing

10.   Issues analysis with the SDLC team

11.   Converting the identified issues into defects.

12.   Recording the defects.

Let us assume the above test schedule items have been planned for 1st test cycle only along with the other tasks [those are not mentioned here].

In reality; assume they are defined further in detail for an ATM testing; the start and the end dates are planned. This test schedule can be announced. It should be communicated to the relevant stakeholders and also to the SDLC teams.

If the testing team finds any of the issues it can be tracked, where they got struck also with these minor tasks tracking. Consider in the earlier sections mentioned example on ATM defects, those can be applied easily and can be tracked for the above test schedule also.

Plan for test staffing:

Assuming you have not yet planned for the required staff. This specific process advises on planning for the required staff. When the management plans the staff, they need to assure the planned team members are aware of the product functionality along with the experience in testing of software products.

Even after hiring or planned them we need to train them on this test project or a particular software release to make sure they understand the latest product requirements and they are capable enough to plan for identifying the decomposable test items also.

As we have discussed in the previous sections, we need to plan for continuous team members orientation on the latest activities and the latest changes incorporating in the software build.

At the same time they also need to be educated by the user teams on their functionalities allocated for test activities.

Example:

If we consider the ATM testing there is couple of sub-functionalities need to be tested. We can plan for different resources to work on those areas or if one person is enough that person need to have complete knowledge on it. At the same time to break the code, the team member needs to have testing experience also. This can help to identify the positive and negative test scenarios to think and plan for various test items.

Note: Please note your high level WBS helps a lot in planning for the staff.

Plan stakeholder involvement:

As we have seen in the previous sections, the stakeholders for the project are the key people. Each of them might play specific role. When they are considered for their involvement on the testing activities, their role, responsibilities need to be defined and should be circulated in advance before the activity or task is started.

Sometimes there can be business sponsors, where they are authority to allocate the budget for the projects. Their involvement is also needed in particular activities to understand and approve the estimated cost.

From project the stakeholders can vary, the management need to identify in the beginning to plan and keep their involvement for different activities.

Example:

Let us assume the ATMs need to be installed once the product is ready to access the customer accounts. The relevant user might think to install the ATMs at different locations by keeping the cameras also. It is a different functionality. Then they might need to plan such environment within the test lab. Their involvement is required for the test lab plan and execution also.

Note:

Assuming the staff or the management has planned the high level WBS. If they are able to allocate the stakeholders along with the staff against to each high level WBS it can give more clarity to the stakeholders and also to the teams.

Identify test project risks

We have established the WBS structure in the previous sections. It doesn't mean that every activity or task can be executed smoothly. In every project there can be issues related to an activity. Those need to be identified through these issues. And risk mitigation can lead to the risk identification.

We have seen in the process of "Analyze product risks". We should consider them towards executing the test activities. And the consolidated risks should be the overall project risks. This way we can identify the test project risks.

Example:

Let us recollect the ATM example we have seen in "Analyze product risks". We also planned to apply the brainstorm by the users to the team members. We need to consolidate those risks to mention under IEEE 829 Test plan document.

This can give clarity to the groups who all are involved and the required support can be availed to resolve the issues/risks. Or even an alternate or contingency plan can be made to move forward with the test activities and to release the product.

Note on project risks: At this stage it is mandatory to maintain a risk register. Regularly the risk register need to be updated and tracked against the open risks. Depends on the capability of the team members a risk checklist can be prepared from the risk register. This can be used to track the latest status of the risk.

Establish the test plan:

We need to develop a test plan document after having all the details of the test planning.

In general, the IEEE 829 template need be used as a standard test plan.

We can see some of the triggered contents through our previous sections for making test plan with the below example.

Example: From the above sections discussions and from their examples,

The typical test plan contents can be:

1.   Test plan identifier

2.   Introduction

3.   Non-compliances with the test strategy

4.   Items to be tested and not to be tested

5.   Features to be tested and not to be tested

6.   Test approach

7.   Entry and exit criteria

8.   Suspension and resumption criteria

9.   Test milestones and work products

10.   Test life-cycle and tasks

11.   Environmental needs and requirements

12.   Staffing and training needs

13.   Stakeholders and their involvement

14.   Test estimates

15.   Test schedule

16.   Test project risks and contingencies

17.   Test project constraints

18.   Test team organization

The analysis we have done through the previous sections are the inputs to the above contents documentation. In each of the previous sections analysis, we should be able to get some documentation also. Those also can be used to fill the above contents.

Let us note as we have discussed in the previous sections the test plan is very essential tool to communicate to all the project relevant teams. And it should be maintained to keep latest updates in this document.

And its circulation and the timely approvals from the require people should be obtained for its baseline.

Chapter 8: Obtain Commitment to the Test Plan

We have seen in many of the above sections on different ways to identify the required testable units and the team orientation along with the users and stakeholders involvement. And we also have worked to create the required test strategy, items to be tested, etc.. and communication on test plan to the relevant groups.

After having all of them in place with all the relevant groups related to the testing project, we should be in a position to get the commitment for the Test plan. It means as the example test plan contents given we have developed the test plan and it was circulated to communicate. Now we need the commitment from the involved teams.

If we get the commitment, whenever the testing gets an issue it should be circulated. The committed people can forward to support the testing team to resolve the issue.

As per the TMMi practices of Test planning process, this goal has the below specific processes:

Review test plan

Reconcile work and resource levels

Obtain test plan commitments

Now let us see each of them.

Review test plan:

Once the test plan is defined, it should be circulated to review and approve by the relevant groups. This approval can denote their understanding and commitments to support the testing activities, issues, resources, etc.

During the review there can be comments. The comments can related to several areas of the test plan contents or the estimates, resources, risks, test approach, identified items for testing, etc. These need to be considered for adopting in test planning activity under process improvement and also for the relevant different test activities. The team members need to be committed on the new updates.

Reconcile work and resource levels:

In many testing projects the test coverage can vary. This variation can be an increase effort or decrease efforts to the resources. When these changes happens, the test planning activity need to be applied from the beginning till the end to make the relevant changes in all. Then the new work need to be reconciled and resources leveling need to be in the project. These are the general project management standards where the test management would know it.

Once these changes are applied or during its apply the relevant groups need to be communicated for their awareness. That can make smooth functioning of the project.

Example:

If you consider the ATM example; Sometimes the test coverage can reduce or it can increase also due to users 11th hour thoughts on test strategy. Then it needs to be reconciled for updates.

Obtain test plan commitments:

We have been observing different stakeholders involvement at different stages of the project. We also made the test plan circulation and got the approvals for the updated contents and for the latest process improvements also.

In this case, we also need to get the commitments from different groups to execute the latest test plan.

Sometimes, we need to refer to the test policies also to make a particular group's involvement.

Example:

While implementing ATM scenarios, we need the network team's support and the ISP provider support apart from the regular project teams or groups. When we seek the network team support the organization test policy might have been defined for the network team's involvement. We should quote those for their involvement.

Conclusion:

By following the above practices with the given feasible example scenarios one can implement these practices in their testing projects incrementally to gain the software quality acceleration under Test planning process.

Let us have a common understanding no new process can be implemented overnight. It need some time to groom the resources, build the test organization by incorporating lot of policies, procedures, standards and processes. Then the internal motivation is also need to be accelerated the speed of the teams. Mainly the management continuous and constant support is required along with the relevant budget. Then the test management can step down to prove the implementation of these best practices incrementally with dedication and long term commitments. If you are satisfied with my elaborations on the specific processes, please look for my other process area books under TMMi level2.

About the author

Shanthi Kumar Vemulapalli is a seasoned professional with 25+ years of global IT experience in cost-effectively utilizing technology in alignment with corporate goals. Delivered bottom-line ITSM results through competent project and program management solutions, successful development and execution of systems, and implementation of best practices. He worked in different BI evaluation phases for more than 10 plus years for different business and technologies domain areas along with 15 years of his involvement in QA/Testing projects.

Recognized for inculcating a culture of innovation and knowledge sharing in organizations. Built teams for many companies globally; through training, mentoring and guiding the IT resources along with the on project competencies building. Supported for many infrastructure setups and conversion related projects [onsite/offshore model].

His Professional Certifications: ITIL V3 Expert Certification –
Service Lifecycle, PRINCE2 Practitioner Certification, Lean
Six Sigma Black Belt, Cloud computing Foundation [EXIN] and
Certified Tester Foundation Level [CTFL].

He also wrote several blogs on the IT related topics. They are
available in the below blog sites:

1. http://vskumarblogs.wordpress.com/

2.http://vskumarcloudblogs.wordpress.com/

3.http://vskumar35.wordpress.com/

Other publications by: Shanthi Kumar Vemulapalli

1. Test planning with TMMi practices

2. How to control cost for IT services - Startup company

3. Testing BI and ETL Applications with manual and
automation approach

4. Data migration testing practice

5. Startup IT Business Ideas: How to strategize your services through ITIL V3 Service Strategy?

6. IT services Design and practices for IT Startup Company

7. IT services Design and practices for IT Startup Company

From the following link also you can see his publications:

http://www.amazon.com/-/e/B018EDQTX6

https://www.createspace.com/pub/simplesitesearch.search.do?sitesearch_query=Shanthi+Kumar&sitesearch_type=STORE